Hippodrome

Tel. Bos. 362381.   **BOURNEMOUTH**   An F.J.B. Theatre

Direction : F. J. Butterworth.   Resident Manager : J. Tomkinson.
Box Office 10 a.m. to 8 p.m.

Week Commencing Monday, Nov. 10th.

6-20 ———— TWCE NIGHTLY ———— 8-30

JOE WAXMAN PRESENTS THE ALL COMEDY FAMILY SHOW

SANDY LANE

YORKSHIRE RELISH

PACK UP

VALANTYNE NAPIER

Presenting

THE HUMAN SPIDER

PATRICIA JOYCE

The Golden Voiced Soprano

★ SONNY LANE

YOUR

TROUBLES

SHIRLEY JEAVONS

A FAMILY AFFAIR

THE MERRY MARTINS

★

★

★

AL BRANDON

Larry Gordon GIRLS
Beauty and Precision

The Voice That Counts

The BENDETTIS

Central Printing Co., (Chas. Sowden) Ltd., Burnley, Lancs.

GLOSSARY OF TERMS USED IN

VARIETY

VAUDEVILLE, REVUE
& PANTOMIME

1880 – 1960

Compiled by Valantyne Napier
with technical advice from Jeff Jones, former Resident
Stage Manager of The Theatre and Opera House,
Cheltenham Spa, Gloucestershire, England

Foreword by Lord Delfont

A contribution from the sale of each copy of this book will be passed to Brinsworth
House, the rest home for retired Variety and Circus artistes, run by The Entertainment
Artistes Benevolent Fund.

Acknowledgements

Thanks are due to Lady Delfont for her kindness in allowing us to reproduce the fine portrait of her late husband which appears with the Foreword.

I am extremely grateful to Ralph Samuels, the Managing Editor of World Acrobatics magazine for providing the majority of the photographs depicting acrobatic and other acts which we have used in this book.

More fascinating details of her career on the Variety stage appear in Valantyne Napier's earlier book "ACT AS KNOWN", published by Globe Press of Melbourne in 1986. Bibliography ISBN 0 9588543 1 9. Copies may still be available through: Ken Pryse & Associates Pty. Ltd., 180 Coventry Street, South Melbourne, Victoria 3205, Australia.

This book is about the lives of the speciality acts. It is about the theatres, the agents, the special theatrical accommodation, the travel and the institutions which once served the enormous commercial enterprise that was the great world of Variety.

GLOSSARY OF TERMS USED IN VARIETY,
VAUDEVILLE, REVUE & PANTOMIME 1880–1960

© Nicholas Charlesworth, 1996
The Badger Press, Westbury, Wiltshire BA13 4DU U.K.

ISBN 0 9526076 5 4

FOREWORD

(Photograph by kind permission of Lady Delfont)

Until television provided entertainment in almost every home in the 1960's, families got their weekly entertainment from a visit to their local Variety, or as it was called in America and some other countries, Vaudeville theatres. Almost every town had one and many towns had three Vaudeville/Variety theatres.

The great entrepreneurs, Oswald Stoll and Edward Moss built chains of elaborately decorated and well equipped Variety theatres from 1880 to 1912 and thousands of skilled artistes, musicians, management staff, stage staff, agents, bookers and providers of theatrical accommodation were employed in this immense profession until television displaced live entertainment at the end of the fifties. There were similar strings of theatres, in America, Australia, New Zealand, South Africa and other countries.

The family entertainment provided in Variety and Vaudeville came from all over the world. Acts of great skill, novelty and spectacle brought laughter, wonder and joy to audiences.

Performers toured the world working, for they always "worked" never "played", the large Vaudeville/Variety circuits. B.F. Keith and Orpheum in America, Rickards and Fuller in Australasia and Moss and Stoll in Britain.

It was a very special world and those "in the business" as it was called, for indeed it was a business, no government subsidies in those days, used a language which is almost lost. A language of "cod acts", "calls", "limes" and many other terms no longer known.

This glossary of terms and some personal explanations has been compiled by a performer who was raised in the profession and was one of the acts represented by my agency.

Her husband, Jeff Jones, former Resident Stage Manager of The Theatre and Opera House, Cheltenham, has provided technical assistance to provide this book which will be a valuable source for historians and students of the theatre.

Lord Delfont   June 1994

Valantyne Napier   Jeff Jones

Photographs by Jacqueline Mitelman, 1992

INTRODUCTION

Since retirement I have been surprised by the number of enquiries I have received regarding terms which have been part of my vocabulary all my life. It was only when it came to explaining to folk who were not, nor had ever been, "in the business" that I realized pros spoke a special language.

It was suggested that this special language be set down in print in order that a record be available after the passing of those few of us remaining from the great days of Vaudeville, or Variety as it was known in Britain.

It is written in the way pros talked and thought. The use of capital letters was the norm for Variety in our day. We thought in capitals. Everything in our profession was larger than everyday life.

We said rostrums, not rostra and bills, NEVER posters! Ever heard of anyone being "top of the poster"? I hope historians and students will try to use our language when they speak of our profession and NOT use the language of television and refer to speciality acts as sight acts. Ventriloquists were speciality acts but could not be categorized as sight acts!

I am greatly indebted to RALPH SAMUELS, Editor of WORLD ACROBATICS for providing the many photographs of various speciality acts used in this book.

Valantyne Napier

NAPIER'S GUIDE TO POPULAR THEATRE BEFORE TV

SHOWS *WITHOUT* CHORUS GIRLS AND NO PRODUCERS, DIRECTORS or TITLES

MINSTREL SHOWS
1830 - 1890

Began in the U.S.A. with Thomas D. Rice in 1830. All male show of plantation songs and dances. Black-faced troupe with white-faced interlocutor or middleman. Six 'endmen' who played the bones and tambourines. First part songs and gags, second part condensed Variety or 'olio', third part 'after-piece'. Used in other countries including Australia.

Potted version on Fullers circuit as second half of program with Vaudeville bill for first half, or vice versa.

Modern version with chorus girls made popular by BBC TV series The Black & White Minstrel Show.

MUSIC HALL
1830 - 1906

Began in the U.K. in pubs and taverns. Later special halls built adjacent to pubs. First claimed as The Star Music Hall 1832 at Bolton, Lancs. Charles Morton's Canterbury Music Hall in London, 1852.

Up to twenty individual 'turns' introduced by a 'Chairman' who also kept control of the boisterous audience. Each 'turn' was quite separate. They did not appear together on stage at any time. There was no 'finale' as shown on the BBC series The Good Old Days.

Music Hall in Australia is said not to have enjoyed the same popularity as in the U.K. The 'halls' were little more than pot-shops where bedraggled performers whose theatrical days were over 'sang and danced' between drinks. (Irvin, 206)

VARIETY
1880 - 1960

A superior form of Music Hall to attract mixed audiences from every strata of society. Began in 1880 when Oswald Stoll and Edward Moss decided to build their large and palatial 'Palaces of Variety' throughout Britain. Eight to ten individual 'acts' of diverse type presented in rapid succession without announcement. There was no compere or 'Chairman'. The acts did not at any time appear together on stage. There was no finale as seen in Royal Variety Shows today. Variety and Music Hall ran side by side from 1880 to 1906 by which time it was all Variety. In Australia the term Vaudeville was used but was synonymous.

Since 1960 The London Palladium has staged mainly Revues & Musicals with only occasional short seasons of Variety.

VAUDEVILLE
1880 - 1932

The Same as Variety in the U.K. Began in the U.S.A. when Tony Pastor decided to present a 'variety of acts suitable for wives, mothers and sisters of the patrons'. First to use the term 'Vaudeville is said to have been John W. Ransome in 1880 but it was Tony Pastor in 1882 who presented 'clean, polite Vaudeville' although he personally preferred the term 'Variety'.

Seven or eight acts of great diversity and skill without interruption or announcement. As in Variety each act was quite separate and speciality acts of every description made up the greater part of the bill.

Jugglers, magicians, tumblers, balancers, animal acts, dancers eccentric, toe or tap, musicians, escapologists, contortionists and a host of others. Novelty was the greatest attraction.

Vaudeville died in 1932 when talkies closed the theatres.

SHOWS *WITH* CHORUS GIRLS, SHOW GIRLS, PRODUCERS, DIRECTORS AND A TITLE

HONKY TONK 1830s - 1890s	BURLESQUE 1869 - 1942	REVUE 1830 - 1996	FOLLIES 1886 - 1996	MUSICAL COMEDY 1866 - 1996
Term applied to dancehalls, saloons & dime museums on the Barbary Coast, U.S.A. where gambling, crime and prostitution flourished. Sleazy comedy, chorus girls of little talent, soubrettes and female impersonators. Eventually grew into night clubs and cabaret.	American style of coarse comedy, bump & grind dancers and one or two fourth rate speciality acts which were not good enough to get into Vaudeville. Burlesque was described by Supreme Court Justice Aaron J. Levey as 'inartistic filth' when he closed down Minsky's in New York in April, 1942. The show Sugar Babies was based on Minsky's Burlesque.	Originally satirical reviews of current news and entertainment in Paris and London. Developed into song and dance shows around 1912 with chorus girls, show girls, topical sketches, several scenes based on a loose theme and with a title to the show. One or two good speciality acts so that the show could be called 'A Variety Revue' or 'Vaudeville Revue' but definitely not Variety or Vaudeville. Tivoli & Fuller shows after June 1931 were Revues. Roy Rene 'Mo', George Wallace and Jim Gerald were Revue comics.	A form of Revue but with the emphasis on beautiful girls, nude or scantily clad. Theme, if any, very loose. Great spectacle, lots of feathers, mirrors etc. A well known comic or singer appearing in several scenes. One or two good speciality acts. Typical shows of this type Ziegfeld Follies and Follies Bergere still running in Paris.	Developed out of Burletta or Light Opera in Vienna, London and New York. Musical song and dance scenes linked by a story or 'book'. Boy and girl dancers and singers. First show definitely classified as a Musical Comedy said to be 'The Black Crook', New York 1866. From 1971 the shows have had more drama and less comedy and are now called 'Musicals' e.g. 'West Side Story', 'Sound of Music', 'Les Miserables'.

Hemp lines and cleats on the fly gallery at The Hackney Empire, London (stage left, looking downstage), seen in August, 1988.

This famous Variety Theatre, designed by Frank Matcham and opened in 1901 for the impresario Oswald Stoll, reopened for live shows in 1987 after many years as a television studio, wrestling venue and bingo hall. It has three circles and retains its fine plasterwork, being one of the largest theatres in London.

© Photograph by kind permission of Ted Bottle

A.A.	The Agents' Association Ltd., founded in London in 1927. President Ernest Edelsten, Vice-Presidents George Foster and George M. Slater.
ACROBATIC ACTS	Many different types of *Acrobatic Acts* worked in Vaudeville/Variety. e.g. *Aerial, Balancing, Bar, Knock-about, Perch, Risley, Teeterboard, Tumbling, Wire*, etc. (see under particular type). From 1900 to 1950s many *Acrobatic Acts* were created specifically for the stage and did not come from the circus.
ACT	Divisions of a play or musical comedy are known as acts but in Vaudeville and Variety, *acts* were quite separate, self-contained performances with no connection to any other part of the programme. An "*Act*" is a performer or group of performers in Vaudeville or Variety. There were usually eight to ten quite diverse Acts on a Vaudeville/Variety programme.
ACT AS KNOWN	The way in which a *Standard Act* was described on a Vaudeville/Variety contract. A "*Standard*" act was an act accepted on the No 1 Circuits around the world and would be booked on reputation "*As known*" without first being seen.
A.C.U.	Actors Church Union. An organization of the Anglican Church in Britain for all members of the theatrical profession. For an annual subscription of 2/6 a list of accommodation which had been checked out by the local vicar was available to performers. A boarding school for children of performers was also available and the local vicar visited the theatres backstage to talk to performers and to provide spiritual help if required.

ADAGIO ACT A slow, controlled and graceful combination of *dance, acrobatic, balancing* and lifting movements usually performed by one male and one female. Sometimes performed with bodies painted gold, bronze or with finely ground mirror particles. e.g. The Diamondos.

ADAGIO ACT

Ruth Hasse and the Ramon Brothers, 1950s   *The Diamondos, 1920s–1940s*

AD LIB To use words or business in a performance which are not part of scripted or usual Act. This would not be permissible on No 1 Circuits and would be a breach of contract.

AERIAL ACT

Trapeze or *Flying Act*, or any other act working in the air above the stage. The equipment for such Acts had to be fixed to the grid above the stage, by the performers, when they arrived at the theatre.

AERIAL ROPE: *Olga Varona*

SINGLE TRAPEZE ACT: *Olga Varona, 1930s–1950s*

AERIAL ACTS

DOUBLE TRAPEZE ACT: *Voltings Star, 1932*

SINGLE TRAPEZE ACT: *Hanni Garden, 1925*

A.F.A.	Actors Federation of Australia registered 6 March 1920. Affiliated with the Variety Artistes' Federation in the U.K.; The Actors and Artists' Association of America and the Union Syndicate des Artists Lyriques of France. The rooms of the A.F.A. were at the Southern Cross Hall, 197 Castlereagh Street, Sydney.
A.F.S.E.A.	Australian Federated Stage Employees' Association registered under the Commonwealth Conciliation and Arbitration Act 1904 on 10th February 1910. It became The Australian Theatrical and Amusement Employees' Association on 15th August 1912. See A.T.A.E.A.
AGENT	It was necessary to have a theatrical *Agent* to negotiate for one's act in America, Britain and on the Continent. The large circuits would not deal directly with acts. In Australia, New Zealand and South Africa, acts could deal directly with the head of the theatre chain e.g. with Harry Rickards or Ben Fuller. Agents usually received ten per cent of the artistes' salary as their fee, hence they were also known as Ten Per Centers.
ANGEL	A financial backer of a theatrical enterprize. One who puts money into the production of a show, usually a big Musical or Revue, e.g. The Ziegfeld Follies. The first known usage of the term was in 1891 in America.
ANIMAL ACTS	The most popular *Animal Acts* in Vaudeville/Variety were Dog Acts e.g. Gautier's Bricklayers; *Chimpanzee Acts* e.g. Dash's Chimpanzees and *Seal Acts* e.g. Odiva's Seals or Olly Olsen and his Sea Lions.

ANTIPODESTA   Another name for a *Contortionist* usually applied to a forward bender rather than a back bender.

ANTIPODESTA

A.N.U.   The Actors National Union in America which opposed The White Rats but were forced to amalgamate with them on the 7 November, 1910 as the White Rats Actors Union.

APOSTERISE   Another name for a *Contortionist* popular around 1900 to 1910. Usually referring to males.

ARAB ACT   A very fast *Tumbling Act* in the Arab style which was a looser type tumbling. Lots of side somersaults, pyramid building etc. Usually quite large troupes.

ARAB ACT
The Charafien Troupe, 1950s

ARTISTE

A professional performer in Vaudeville or Variety. Performers referred to themselves as "Pros" being short for professionals, or as *Artistes*. They never used the term "Actor" or "Actress".

A.T.A.E.A.

Australian Theatrical and Amusement Employees' Association, founded 15th August 1912. Amalgamated in 1992 with Australian Actors Equity.

A.T.T.

African Theatres Trust Ltd.

AUDITION

To give a performance of one's acting, singing or dancing ability before producers etc., without an audience. Vaudeville and Variety artistes did not have to give auditions. They usually obtained a "Showdate" or went on at a "Trial Night" before an audience where their audience appeal could be gauged. See *Showdates* and *Trial Nights*.

A.V.A.A.

Australian Vaudeville Artists' Association officially opened 9th May, 1907, in Sydney. President Bert Rache occupied the chair with an attendance of 200. Sam Gale had recently founded a similar institution in Melbourne. It failed through lack of members in 1911. Most visiting performers belonged to the professional organizations in their country of origin. e.g. the V.A.F. in the U.K. or N.V.A. in U.S.A.

A.V.A.F.

Australian Vaudeville Artiste's Federation formed 1912. This organization also failed to attract sufficient members to survive and failed around 1920. The A.F.A. was then formed.

BACKSTAGE

All the area of a theatre behind the footlights and fire-curtain, including dressing rooms, scene dock, flys, stagedoor etc. The resident Stage Manager was in complete authority over everything backstage including electricians.

BADMINTON ACTS

Displays of badminton interspersed with acrobatic tricks enjoyed quite a vogue in Variety in the late 40s. They were also featured in Ice Shows.

BALANCE

The arrangement of a programme, for Vaudeville or Variety in such a way as to give the greatest diversity of acts, e.g. only one *Comic*, one *Singer*, one *Dancing Act*, one *Acrobatic Act*, one *Juggling Act*, one *Magic Act*, one *Ventriloquist*, one *Skating Act* etc; also a balance between full stage acts and front cloth acts to ensure the smooth running of high speed changes from one act to the next.

BALANCING ACTS

All types of *Balancing Acts* were popular in Vaudeville/Variety. Hand to hand; hand to head; head to head; head or hand on all sorts of props; balancing swords or cannons on the forehead; balancing on toes in pointe shoes along the tops of a row of beer bottles, *Roller Balancing*, etc.

♪ HEAD BALANCING: *Ted Weeks of Vyne & Valantyne, 1940s & 50s*

HAND TO HEAD BALANCING: ♪
Homer & Hal, 1950s

BALANCING ACTS

FEET TO HEAD BALANCING: ☞
*Vyne & Valantyne, 1940s–1950s
(Photograph was taken from the wings at the METROPOLITAN, Edgware Road)*

BALANCING ACTS *(continued)*

✎ HAND TO HAND BALANCING: *Renald & Rudy, 1956*

♪ HEAD TO HEAD BALANCING, THREE HIGH:
The Namedil Brothers, 1940s

BALL BOUNCERS   A type of *Juggling Act* popular 1905-1925.

BALL BOUNCERS
Decima Martyn working Collins' Music Hall

BALLOON ACT   Making animals and other novelties from balloons enjoyed quite a vogue in the 1950s.

BAND ACTS	Many famous *Bands*, of all types from Sousa to Jack Hylton, performed Vaudeville/Variety Acts. There were several excellent Comedy Bands e.g. Billy Cotton; The Nitwits; Dr Crock & his Crackpots: also *Bands* of particular instruments e.g. Troise and his Mandoliers; Borah Minevitch Harmonica Players; etc. Also all Female Bands e.g. Ivy Benson Band. The bands usually took up most of the second half of the programme.
BANDCALL	The rehearsal of an acts' music with the resident *Musical Director* and pit orchestra. Vaudeville/Variety Acts were required to provide all necessary band parts. Musicians in pit orchestras were great sight readers and could play even complicated scores perfectly at sight. The acts did not perform for rehearsals. They merely listened to the music to ensure correct tempos and to give cues. Bandparts were placed near the footlights and taken in the order placed without regard to position on the bill. The top of the bill took their turn in the same way as the smallest act on the bill.
BANDPARTS	Every act in Vaudeville or Variety was required to have a full set of band parts for the music used in their act. The number of parts needed depended on the size of the pit orchestra. On the No 1 Variety circuits this was from seventeen to twenty-one. On No 2 circuits from eight to eleven. In Vaudeville in America, the pit orchestras were smaller and in many theatres only five to eight parts were needed. The parts required were usually Conductor, three violins, cello, bass, three trumpets, two trombones, three or four saxophones, piano, percussion, clarinet and for Panto a harp part! If acts were working constantly two shows a day, six or seven days a week, the band parts soon became worn and torn so new parts were needed at least every year. It was not unknown for musicians to write messages or their critique of the act on the bandparts for the musicians at the next theatre!!!

BANDROOM   A dressingroom, usually under the stage, where the pit orchestra changed or retired to when not required to play for an act. e.g. During a *Patter Act*.

BAR ACT   *Horizontal Bar Act.* Two or three horizontal bars were usually used with spectacular acrobatics from, and over and under the bars. Great scope for comedy.

BAR ACT

HORIZONTAL BARS: *Los Cristesco, 1937*

BARRING CLAUSE   A clause in a Vaudeville/Variety contract prohibiting the act appearing in another theatre within a certain radius for a certain time, usually six months.

BATTENS   Lengths of timber to which the tops of cloths and borders were tied. The battens were raised by sets of three lines from the flys. Some acts tied apparatus to battens.

BEARER   The under stand or acrobat who supports the top mount in a *Balancing* or *Perch Act*.

BENDER Another name for a *Contortionist*, usually a *Backbender*. Regarded as slightly derogatory and often used by *Comics* in that sense.

BENDER

Lena, 1950s

BIG TIME The two a day Vaudeville in America and Canada. The Orpheum and B.F. Keith circuits.

BILL The placards pasted on hoardings to advertise the acts on the programme at theatres. Artistes always referred to "being on the bill" never on the programme. Today bills are often erroneously referred to as posters. The "posters" or "pasters" were the men who pasted the *Bills* on the hoardings. There were over 700 members of the United Bill Posters' Association in Britain in 1917. The size of bills was expressed in terms of the number of sheets of paper in a bill. e.g. "A Six Sheeter", "A Twelve Sheeter" or "A Twenty Four Sheeter".

BILLBOARD The hoarding on which *Bills* were posted or pasted. Also the name of a famous American weekly theatre newspaper.

VARIETY BILL, 1949

VAUDEVILLE BILL

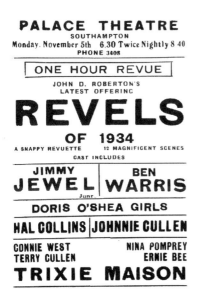

REVUE BILL, 1934

PANTOMIME BILL, 1953-4

BILLING | The size of the print and the position on the bill in relation to other acts. Very important to the acts as dressingrooms were allocated according to the *Billing*. The top of the bill got No 1 dressingroom. If there were three acts sharing *Top* the one on the left got No 1 then centre got No 2 and the act on the right No 3. Next the act or acts on the bottom of the Bill. Then the middle of the *Bill* and then the others according to space and size of print. Dressingrooms were allocated by the resident Stage Manager unless special instructions were received from Head Office of a circuit.

BILL MATTER | In addition to the name of the act there was a descriptive word or phrase identifying the act. e.g. "Noveloddities" was the bill matter for Vyne & Valantyne; "Australia's Queen of The Air" was the Bill Matter for Olga Varona and "Cleopatra's Nightmare" was the bill matter for Wilson, Keppel and Betty.
Bill Matter was copyright and could not be used by another act.

BILLS NEXT WEEK | Columns in American theatrical trade papers, e.g. "Variety" and "Billboard", which listed the names of all the Vaudeville Theatres and the acts booked for the next week.

BITS | Short comedy interludes much used in Revues and Pantomimes usually ending with a blackout. Often well known set pieces e.g. "Interruptions".

BLACKOUT | A sudden switch-off of all stage lighting and limes. Used for effect at end of gag or scene. Mostly used in Revues or Pantomime. One switch controlled all circuits on the board but it was important that all lights backstage and in the flies were extinguished.

BLUE STUFF | Suggestive or risque material was prohibited. There were warnings in dressingrooms and the curtain could be dropped on any act not heeding the warning.

B.O.	Blackout. See above.
BOOKER	Person responsible for booking the acts for the large Vaudeville/Variety circuits, e.g. B.F. Keith and Orpheum in America or Moss and Stoll in Britain. Some well known *Bookers* were women. e.g. Cissie Williams for Moss Empires and Florence Leddington for the Syndicate dates. In Australasia acts usually dealt directly with the owner of the circuit but when Ben Fuller was overseas, Walter J. Douglas operated as *Booker* for Fullers.
BORDERS	Short cloths or drapes hung to mask or hide light battens or tops of cloths from the audience.
BOUNCE IT	In use in Australia and N.Z. after 1960, meaning to drop house Tabs or curtain and take up again immediately for applause at end of Revue or show. Not used in Vaudeville or Variety or known elsewhere.
BOX OFFICE	Booth at front of theatre where patrons booked their seats from a box office plan.
BRACE	Two pieces of adjustable wood with a hook on one end to affix to scenery and a bracket on the other end to hold in place on the stage with a heavy stage weight. See illustration.

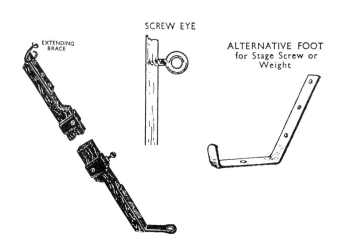

SCREW EYE

ALTERNATIVE FOOT
for Stage Screw or
Weight

EXTENDING
BRACE

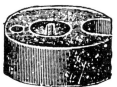

BRACE WEIGHT

BUMPING IN	A term now in use in Australia for *Getting In* or *Getting Out* theatre scenery, props, trunks, baskets etc. In Britain the terms used are still "Getting In" and "Getting Out". There are special rates for "Get Ins," and "Get Outs" set in the awards for backstage staff.
BURLESQUE 1	A satire on a popular play in seventeenth or eighteenth century English Theatre.
BURLESQUE 2	1869-1942. Also called "Burley" or "Burleycue". American low comedy and sex shows mainly for men. Chorus girls of little dancing ability, several low comedians, the lead of which was termed "Top Banana", strippers and bump and grind dancers. The famous or infamous Minsky's Burlesque in New York was closed down in April 1942 by court order being described as "inartistic filth" by the judge. The 1980s Musical "Sugar Babies" was based on Burlesque. See Napiers' Guide to Popular Theatre Before T.V.
BURLESQUE 3	Some acts in Vaudeville/Variety based their acts on a Burlesque or take-off of another well known act.
BUSINESS	Comedy actions, walks, postures, facial expressions etc., which could form known part of an act. e.g. Charlie Chaplain's walk and cane; Max Wall's piano routine; or the Bashful Boys' tangle routine with coats.
CALL	*Taking a Call* was receiving applause for one's act. Amateurs say "taking a bow". Pros did not bow. They stood with arms outstretched to receive the applause, looked up to the gallery, then circle and to the stalls, acknowledged the *Musical Director* and pit orchestra, particularly the drummer, and then exited to the wings. Bowing is usually only seen when Royalty is present in the audience or by Concert Artists, Orchestral or Ballet performers.

CALL BOY	Before loud-speaker systems were introduced in theatre dressingrooms, young boys were employed to knock on dressingroom doors and call the artistes when it was time for them to go on stage. In the 40s most theatres had speaker systems in dressingrooms so acts could hear what was going on on the stage and take their cues or the Stage Manager could call them over the system. Very few theatres employed *Call Boys* in the 1940s and 50s. Also the name of the quarterly magazine of The British Music Hall Society.
CALLS	The half hour, fifteen minute, five minute and overture beginners *Calls* made by the Stage Manager to warn acts of the time before the curtain up.
CALLS, THE	Columns in British theatrical papers e.g. "The Stage", "Performer" and "Show World" which listed all Variety Theatres and the names of acts booked for the next week. (see also "Bills Next Week")
CATCHER	The *Acrobat* who catches the *Flyer* in a *Flying Act* or *Teeter-Board Act*.
CHORUS BOYS	Male singers and dancers in Musical Comedy or Revue. Usually equal numbers with chorus girls.
CHORUS GIRLS	There were no chorus girls in Vaudeville or Variety. There were individual Dancing Acts of maybe two or three girls, or boys or even a troupe of *Speciality Dancers* e.g. The Tiller Girls or The Ballet Montmarte, but they were separate acts and only performed their own spot on the programme. Chorus girls belonged in Revues and Musical Comedy, where they might make as many as eight appearances in different costumes to provide a background to principals in *Scenas* etc. Chorus girls in Australasia were called "Ballet Girls" although few were accomplished in classical Ballet.

17

CINE-VARIETY

In the 1920s, 30s and 40s some cinemas put on a few acts, usually *Specialities*, before the pictures. Cine-variety provided the main source of employment for many acts after Vaudeville Theatres closed and Variety was struggling due to the "talkies".

CLEAT

A metal or wooden fixture on scenery or on the *Fly Rail* to which ropes were fixed. See illustration.

CLEAT-LINE

A piece of sash cord attached to a *Flat* which was used to secure it to another *Flat* by means of fixing on the *Cleat*. See illustration.

TOP OF
TWO ADJOINING FLATS

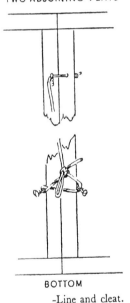

BOTTOM
-Line and cleat.

—Throwline cleat.

CLOSE IN ONE

An act which could open or close their act well downstage in what was called "One", i.e. the first opening beyond the footlights before the first set of wings helped the rapid pace of a Vaudeville/ Variety programme. A good Booker tried to balance the Bill with acts which could open or close in "One".

CLOTHS

Large sheets of painted canvas hung from battens to display a scene. Street scenes were used for *Comics*; ballroom scenes might be used for *Dancing Acts*; wood scenes for some *Speciality Acts*. Scenic Artists who painted the cloths were highly skilled and the scenes were most realistic. See Paint Frame.

COD ACT

A pretence or hoax act. e.g. A Cod Magic Act pretends to disclose the way the tricks are done. A Cod Boxing Bout may be just a knockabout acrobatic Act.

COMBINED ROOM

A combined bedroom/dining/sittingroom. The most usual form of accommodation in theatrical digs.

COMIC

A *Comedian* or *Comedienne*.

COMMISSION NOTE

An agreement to pay the *Agents'* commission was signed for every week or period of an engagement.

COMPERE

Someone to introduce acts on amateur shows, trial nights and later radio and television or in Revues. There were no *Comperes* in Vaudeville or Variety. In the early days the acts were announced by boards on an easel on the side of the stage. From the thirties acts were signified by numbers in lights on the proscenium and reference to the printed programmes. When business was bad due to the talking pictures, cost cutting measures saw some theatres introduce *Comperes* to cut out a couple of acts.

CONJURER

See *Magic Acts* and *Prestidigitator*. Simple conjuring e.g. pulling rabbits out of hats, belonged more to Club Acts or children's parties.

CONTORTIONIST

A very supple acrobat. See also *Antipodesta* and *Bender*.

CONTRACT

An agreement between the act and theatre management or circuit was drawn up and signed for every week or period of engagement.

COON ACTS   A remnant from Minstrel Shows. Also called Coon Delineators. Numerous in Vaudeville/ Variety 1900-1930. Worked in blackface make-up and sang plantation songs. e.g. Eugene Stratton and G.H. Elliot.

CUES   It was necessary to mark all *Cues* on Conductors' *Band Parts*, also to have *Cue Cards* to give to the *Chief Electrician*, *lime boys*, *Stage Manager* etc. These *Cues* denoted when to open or close the *Tabs*, bring the lights up, black out etc.

CUT-OUTS   Borders with legs attached, painted like tree branches and foliage and cut out to shape. Used in wood scenes in Pantomimes, Revues or for some acts in Variety.

CYCLE ACTS   All forms of cycles, some very tiny, many trick cycles and comedy bikes were used in *Cycle Acts*. Anything from solo to ten or more members in troupe.

CYCLE ACT
The 4 Sidney's, 1935

CYCLORAMA	A pale blue, plain cloth, like a sky cloth but curved. Usually hung at the back of the stage on the last set of lines. It gave great depth to scenes and was much used in Pantomimes and by spectacular acts or acts working in silhouette. e.g. Patillo & Pesco; or The Human Spider.
DAME	The main character in Pantomime traditionally played by a male *Comedian*.
DANCING ACTS	An amazing variety of types and styles of *Dancing Acts* performed in Vaudeville/Variety. *Classical Ballet* e.g. Pavlova and Espinosa; *Ballroom* e.g. The Castles and the Astaires; *Specialist Charleston Dancers* e.g. Lew Grade; *Sand Dancers* e.g. Wilson, Keppel and Betty; *Eccentric Dancers* e.g. Ray Bolger; Delfont & Toko; *Tap Dancers* e.g. Danny Lipton or George Murphy; *Acrobatic Dancers* e.g. George Wallace or Donald O'Connor; *Toe-Tappers* e.g. Mahala; etc.
DANSEUSE	A *Toe Dancer* or *Ballerina*. This term was frequently used from 1901 to 1920.
DATE	A booking. Professional Vaudeville/Variety Acts always referred to working "Dates", not bookings.
DATE BOOKS	Small pocket books either provided annually by Artistes' professional associations or by some theatrical trade papers. The weeks of the year were listed with space to enter Bookings or "Dates". The *Date-Books* also contained useful information e.g. Theatre stage door phone numbers; lists of Agents and columns to record expenditure etc.
DEAD	The fix when hanging a scene *Cloth* or *Tabs* so that they just touch the stage and do not leave a gap through which light or feet behind the *Cloth* could be seen by the audience. The fly ropes are "tied off" at the "dead" reached during setting so that when they are dropped in during the performance they will be in exactly the correct position.

DEAD-PAN	To work with an expressionless face. Some acts worked *Dead-Pan* throughout the entire act. Useful for *Acrobatic* or *Juggling Acts* with great skills but not much stage personality.
DEAD STAGE	A stage without any spring in it. Very difficult to work on for *Tumblers* and *Dancers*.
DENTAL ACTS	*Aerial Acts* performed by gripping with the teeth instead of hands or legs.

The Antalias, 1950s　　　　　　　　*The 2 Tulanos, 1951*

DENTAL ACTS

DIABOLO ACTS

Large reels manipulated with string between two hand held sticks. *Diabolo Acts* enjoyed great popularity from around 1914 to the late 20s. Quite spectacular in skilled hands.

DIABOLO ACT

DOUBLE DIABOLO PLAY

DIDDY

Toilet or W.C. The term much used particularly by female performers.

DIE A DEATH

To fail to win audience appreciation. For a *Comic* not to get laughs or for any act to exit with little or no applause.

DIGS

Theatrical accommodation. In Australia, New Zealand, South Africa and parts of America usually hotels which catered specifically for theatricals. There were also many "Pro" boarding houses in America as typified in the book "Are You Decent". In Britain usually private homes which took in Pros. Lists of Digs which had been inspected by the clergy and were recommended by The Actors Church Union could be obtained annually for 2/6. On the Continent it was usual to rent a pension.

DIMMERS

Controls on the main switchboard which operated all circuits to stage lighting in footlights, floods, light battens and dips. The lights could be gradually dimmed by manually controlled handles on the dimmer panels.

DIPS	Small boxes in the floor of the stage containing plugs for the connections of floodlights etc. These were operated from the main switchboard.
DOCK	The section of the stage, either at side or back, where scenery is stored.
DOCK DOORS	The high, wide doors where scenery etc., is loaded into and out of the theatre.
DOWNSTAGE	Towards the footlights. Stages were "raked" i.e. they sloped towards the footlights in order that the feet of performers could be seen even from the front stalls. Therefore "Downstage" was literally down.
DRAMATIC ACTS	Many dramatic actors e.g. Sarah Bernhardt; the Lunts; the Barrymores; G.P. Huntley etc performed in Vaudeville/Variety. See Protean Artistes.
EM-CEE	Master of Ceremonies. Some theatres in America held Amateur Nights or Amateur Weeks and it was necessary to have a Compere or M.C. who was called an "Em-Cee" to introduce the contestants. At the end of the show he walked behind each contestant and held his hand over their head. As he did so the audience showed its appreciation, or otherwise, for each act. The act which won the most applause might then win a professional engagement for the following week. As they were locals they would bring patrons, friends and relatives, to the theatres. It was not usual to have an Em-Cee in Vaudeville but towards the dying days of Vaudeville it was tried in shows which were part-Vaudeville and part-revue. It was not well received by audiences in high speed Vaudeville.
ECCENTRIC DANCER	A looselegged *Dancer* of Funny Walks etc. Also described as *Legmania*.
FEED, A	A comedians' straightman or woman, who feeds the lines to the *Comic*. Also described as a Comic's Labourer.

FESTOON CURTAIN	An undivided curtain with numbers of wires which were controlled by a manual machine offstage to create numerous designs, drapes and festoons. Used to great effect for different settings in Variety.
FINALE	A short final Scena at the end of Pantomime and Revue in which all the artistes walk down to the footlights to receive applause. They take their call in reverse order to their importance. The chorus first, then Principals and by tradition the "Dame" last. A cheery farewell song by the company completes the show before the house curtain. There was no *Finale* in Vaudeville or Variety.
FIRE CURTAIN	A heavy steel and asbestos curtain separating the backstage area from the auditorium. It was required to be lowered and raised before each performance to ensure that it was in working order and to display a plan of emergency exits painted on the fire curtain.
FIREDOORS	All doors from the stage to the dressingrooms and auditorium had to be fireproof and kept closed.
FIRE-EATING	A Sideshow or Circus Act. Not usual in Vaudeville/Variety.
FIREPROOFING	All scenery and props had to be fireproofed. Firemen attended theatres and actually put blow torches to the centre of cloths etc to test that fireproofing was effective. Anything not proofed had to be removed from the theatre and could not be used.
FIT-UP	Another term for setting the stage.
FIT-UPS	Small touring companies which worked in towns which had no real theatres. They used church halls, shearing sheds, barns etc and "Fitted them up" with whatever staging, scenery, curtains etc. they brought with them.
FLASH ACT	In American Vaudeville a two-man Vaudeville act which added a soubrette and a few girls and some scenery to make a bigger presentation of their act.

FLASH-BOX

A box of magnesium powder ignited by an electrical fuse producing a bright flash and smoke. Usually placed near footlights and used to great effect in Pantomime for the appearances of the Demon King. Also used by some *Magic Acts* in Vaudeville/Variety.

FLATS

Single pieces of rigid scenery. They could stand alone, held in place by means of braces and weights or stage screws, or be joined to other flats by means of ropes and cleats. Used in Variety by acts like Lucan and McShane.

FLICKER-WHEEL

A cut out, metal revolving wheel placed in front of spotlight to give impression of greater speed. Used by dancers or acrobats for a "Wow" finish to act.

FLIES

The section of the theatre immediately above the stage from which cloths, scenery, equipment e.g. trapeze and gear used by some acts, was suspended and stored when not in immediate use.

FLOATS

Another name for footlights. In the early use of footlights across the front of the stage, candles in saucers were "floated" in a trough of water.

FLOODS

Abbreviation for floodlights. Rows of floodlights placed around the circle of the theatre flooded the stage with light. There were also floods on the side of the stage, singly or in banks of two or three, placed in the wings. See illustration.

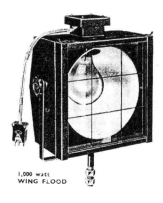

1,000 watt
WING FLOOD

FLYFLOOR	A gallery above the stage, usually on one side, where the flymen worked to carry out the flying of scenery etc. There was a strong rail on the side where the ropes or fly-lines were tied off around large wooden or metal cleats.
FLYING ACT	Trapeze Act with two or more pieces of apparatus and acrobats "flying" from one to another with the aid of "catchers". Not much seen on stage due to amount of space required. Typical Circus act.
FLYMAN	A member of stage staff whose job it was to "fly" and lower scenery suspended in the flies.
FLYER	The acrobat in a Teeter-Board or Flying Act who does the aerial acrobatics and is caught by the catcher.
FOLD	For a show to be taken off due to poor business.
FOLLIES	1886-1990. See Napier's Guide to Popular Theatre Before T.V.
FOOTLIGHTS	A row of lights sunk to stage level on the audience side of the *house tabs* or front curtain. They were set on the oblique to shine upwards. Every fourth light was white, the others had red, blue and amber gelatines or "jellies" in frames so that the stage could be lighted according to the requirements of the acts. Most theatres had replaced gas lighting with electricity by 1905.
FOOTS	A common abbreviation of footlights.
FRENCH BRACE	A hinged piece fitted to a ground row which could be held in place by stage weights. See illustration.
FRONT CLOTH	A cloth hung well downstage in the No 1 entrance. Hence a *Frontcloth Comic* or *Frontcloth Act* is one which works in that small space of the stage. The space depended on the size of the theatre but was usually about ten feet to twelve feet or three metres in depth. See also "Close in one".

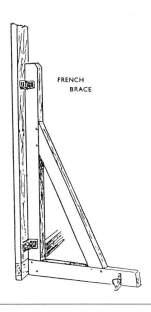

FRENCH
BRACE

FRENCH BRACE

FRONT OF HOUSE	The auditorium, vestibule and booking office all under the control of the Front of House Manager.
FRONT TABS	The front curtain or House Tabs. Often red plush with gold motif of theatre circuit. It could be raised to the flies or parted in the centre and drawn off to the sides.
FULL STAGE	The full extent of the stage available to perform on. Cycle Acts, Acrobatic Troupes, Bar Acts, Magic Acts, Trapeze Acts all required a full stage for their Acts.
FUNAMBULIST	A Rope-Walker. See Wire Walkers.
FULL-UP	A sudden switch on of all stage lighting for effect at end of act to bring applause.
GAGS	Jokes told by a comedian.
GAUZE	A cloth of gauze much used in Pantomimes in revelation scenes. Several gauzes were used and as each one was raised more of a scene was revealed. The gauze gave special effects according to how it was lighted.

GELATINES

Coloured sheets of gelatine placed in wire frames which fitted over lights in spotlights, floods, foots, light battens, towers etc. According to which circuit was used the stage could be coloured, red, white, blue, amber or any other colour desired. The gelatines were identified by numbers e.g. 36 Pale Lavender or Surprise Pink; 20 Deep Blue; 34 Golden Amber.

GET IN/OUT

Get Ins and Get Outs, the technical term for moving scenery, props, trunks, skips etc to and from theatres. In most towns the scenery etc was transported by rail then brought to theatres by theatrical baggage-carriers. Stage hands were sometimes required at the rail depots to handle scenery or to just get it into and out of the theatre onto trucks. Special rates of pay for "Getting In" and "Getting Out" were established in the awards of theatrical employees unions. Some theatres were known as "Difficult Get Ins/Outs" and extra payment applied. Touring shows had to take account of the extra costs involved when working these theatres.

GHOST

"When does the ghost walk" meant what time do the acts get paid. In Two-a Day Vaudeville/ Variety it was during the second house of the last night usually Saturday. It ensured that no act could "skip" or "vamoose" without doing the final performance.

GLOBE ACT

Performers balancing on large spheres and rolling them by moving their feet rapidly. They were rolled around the stage, up ramps, over narrow planks etc.

GLOBE ACT
The Original 4 Livier, 1937

G.O.L.R.	Grand Order of Lady Ratlings, see under Water Rats.
G.O.W.R.	Grand Order of Water Rats, see under Water Rats.
GREASEPAINT	Stage make-up. Sticks of various coloured greasepaint were applied over a coldcream base. The flesh colours most used were Lit K or a mixture of 5 and 9. Males used more 9 which gave a deeper tan appearance. Leichners, the famous brand of greasepaints, became unavailable during World War Two. At this time Max Factor stage make-up, a cream form in tubes became popular with performers. Make-up in Vaudeville/Variety was applied by the performers themselves and was not the exaggerated caricature portrayed in "Lost Empires" and other T.V. series.
GRID	The strong section of the theatre construction, above the stage and the flies, to which the pulleys holding the fly ropes are fixed. *Aerial Acts* had to climb to the *Grid* to affix their apparatus. See illustration.

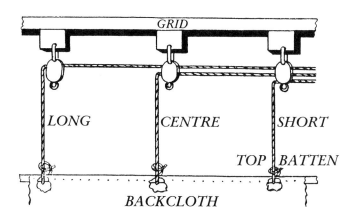

Showing the Long (single) pulley; the Centre (double) pulley; and the Short (three-fold) pulley, with the three lines in position, and the Grid Rail to which they are fixed. This process is employed in 'flying' backcloths or portions of scenery, etc.

GROUNDROW — A low piece of scenery used to mask the front of rostrums, stairs etc. Usually supported by a *French Brace*. Also a row of floodlights on the stage shining upward onto a cloth e.g. *Skycloth* or *Cyclorama*.

GUY ROPES — Ropes or wires used to hold apparatus in position. Used by *Bar Acts, Aerialists* and for special gear e.g. *Spiders Web*. The ropes or wires could be tightened by means of pulleys.

HONKY-TONKS — 1830-1890. See Napier's Guide to Popular Theatre Before T.V.

HOUSE — The term applied to the auditorium, hence a "Full House" meant a full auditorium, or all seats sold.

HOUSE AT HALF — To have the *House Lights* at half strength usually for members of the audience to come up on stage to assist in *Hypnotist* or *Magic Act* or in Panto.

HOUSE LIGHTS — All the lights in the auditorium which were lowered at the commencement of the programme when the Stage Manager signalled "House Lights Down."

HOOFER — Term applied to *Tap Dancer* particularly in America.

HORIZONTAL BAR ACT — See Bar Act.

HYPNOTISTS — During the early fifties Stage Hypnotists enjoyed great popularity. e.g. Peter Casson.

ILLUSIONISTS — Large production acts e.g. Houdini; Chung Ling Soo; Maskelyne; Les Levante etc; who performed big illusions e.g. Sawing Women in Half; Disappearing Lions; Escapes under water etc., toured their own large companies and either took over the whole bill or a large part of it. See also Magicians.

IMPERSONATORS
Male and female Impersonators who made a thorough character study of their subjects so that every movement, mannerism and item of dress was perfect. It wasn't just a matter of donning the attire of the opposite sex. e.g. Vesta Tilley; Hetty King; Ella Shields; Nellie Kolle; Effie Fellowes; or in recent times Danny la Rue and Barry Humphries.

MALE IMPERSONATOR: *Hetty King, during her performance at BRIXTON EMPRESS in 1964 (Courtesy of Maurice Michel)*

FEMALE IMPERSONATOR: *Danny La Rue (Courtesy of Duggie Chapman Associates)*

IMPERSONATORS

IMPRESSIONISTS
Performers who gave vocal impressions of famous people; e.g. Winston Churchill, Hitler or film stars, using few props e.g. Churchill's cigar or Hitler's fringe. This type of act came into vogue after the introduction of microphones in 1933.

JUGGLING ACTS

Everything from feathers to cannon-balls and even water was juggled in acts in Vaudeville/ Variety. From the great Cinquevalli early this century to Rob Murray in the the dying days of Variety, Jugglers were popular Standard Acts.

Decima Martyn seen during her act at COLLINS' MUSIC HALL, Juggling with Clubs, Cigar Boxes and Plates, 1930s–40s

JUMPING ACT

High Jumpers, jumping into and out of barrels etc without the aid of a trampoline or similar device. A popular type of act from 1905 to 1920.

JUVENILE ACTS

Almost every type of act could be performed by juveniles until the Child Welfare Regulations restricted their performances. These regulations differed in various countries and states.

KNAP	Knock or rap. See also Nap and Slapstick. To *Take the Knap* meant one performer slapped their hands loudly when another performer hit them. To the audience it seemed as though the noise came from the hit as the actual hands clapping were concealed. Much used in *Comedy Acrobatic Acts*.
KNAPSTICK	Also called Napstick or Slapstick. Two long, flexible pieces of wood joined together at one end, which gave a loud clap when hit against the hand or body.
KNOCKABOUT	This type of Slapstick was much used by *Comedy Acrobatic Acts*, also by Buster Keaton in films.
LADDER ACTS	Unsupported Ladders were used in many acts for Acrobatic and Juggling feats. Perhaps the most famous Unsupported Ladder Act was Du Calion who balanced atop the Ladder for the duration of his *Patter Act* around 1914. See also Revolving Ladder.

LADDER ACTS

UNSUPPORTED LADDER:
Leopold Kremo, 1955

LEGIT Term used by Vaudeville/Variety Artistes to describe dramatic actors and stage plays etc.

LEGMANIA Looselegged or Eccentric Dancing and Funny Walks.

LIGHT BATTEN Metal battens carrying four circuits of overhead lights. Usually red, blue, white and amber. They were controlled by the switchboard and each circuit could be controlled independently. Most Vaudeville/Variety Theatres had three or four light battens depending on the depth of the stage.

LIGHTNING SKETCH ACTS Artists who could produce likenesses of famous or topical characters with a few deft lines from a brush or pen whilst giving Comedy Patter e.g. Bert Levy; or in later years Rolph Harris.

LIGHTING PLOT The instructions and cues for lighting an act, given to the Chief Electrician.

LIME-BOYS The operators of the Limes or spotlights. The experienced "Lime Boys" could be over 60. A good *Lime-Boy* could follow a fast moving acrobat or focus a pin spot even on moving artistes.

LIME-BOX The small room usually high above the gallery in the auditorium from which the limes or spotlights were operated.

LIMELIGHT Exceptionally bright white light on principal performers. Hence to be "In The Limelight" meant to attract the most attention. See Limes.

LIME PLOT Instructions and cues for an act given to *Lime-Boys*.

LIMES   Spotlights operated from high up in the auditorium, to pick out and follow the Artiste on stage. Originally the intense white light was produced by heating lime in a cylinder in an oxyhydrogen flame. Later carbon rods, which needed priming before the performance, were used. In inexperienced hands the lights could splutter and go out causing great agitation to the Performer left in a blackout!

LINES   The fly ropes in the theatre which were tied to the Battens. The rope on the side nearest the Fly-Floor was called the "Short". The rope farthest away was called the "Long". Hence when the settings were being made it was usual to hear the Stage Manager call to the Fly-Men "Up on your Short, down on your Long", or vice versa, to get the Tabs or Cloths level. The ropes or Lines were then tied off around cleats on the rail of the Fly Floor.

MAGIC ACTS   Everything from a short Front-Cloth Act to a Full Stage Act taking up the whole of the second half of the programme with a large Company. See Illusionists.

MAKE-UP   See Greasepaints. Each Performer in Vaudeville/Variety applied their own *Make-Up*.

MASKING   Keeping all the backstage hidden from the audience. The space above the *Battens* and between the *Cloths*, had to be masked so that the audience did not see the ropes, braces, weights etc. used to hold scenery and so that the performers were not seen preparing for their acts.

MENTAL-TELEPATHY   Mind-reading or Mental Telepathy enjoyed popularity in Vaudeville/Variety from early in the century until the sixties. e.g. Argus, The Boy Wonder; and The Piddingtons.

M.H.A.R.A.   Music Hall Artists' Railway Association founded on 2nd February, 1897 in Britain. It was the oldest organisation connected with the Variety profession. For a small annual subscription it obtained special reduced fares and luggage concessions on railways throughout Britain for the thousands of Variety Acts which travelled by rail from town to town, every Sunday. Changes to British Rail resulted in an end to the organisation in 1953.

MIKES   Microphones. The first microphones to be used in Variety and Revues were installed in the early 1930s. Before that time, Performers could project their voices to all parts of 2000 seat theatres. By the 40s there were stand mikes, riser mikes and foot mikes in almost all Variety Theatres.

MINSTREL SHOWS   1830-1890 See Napier's Guide to Popular Theatre Before T.V.

MUSICAL ACTS   All types from *Accordionists* and *Banjoists* to *Xylophonists* and *Zither Players*. Pianists e.g. Charlie Kunz; Semprini; Ivor Moreton & Dave Kaye; and Winifred Atwell were popular *Tops of Bills*.

MUSICAL ACT

The Merry Martins, 1950s

MUSICAL COMEDY	1866-1971. See Napier's Guide to Popular Theatre Before T.V.
MUSIC HALL	1830-1906. See Napier's Guide to Popular Theatre Before T.V.
N.A.T.K.E.	The National Association of Theatrical and Kine Employees was established in England in 1899 and is the oldest trade union in the profession. It represents the technical, craft and general staff grades employed in all theatres throughout Great Britain.
N.V.A.	National Vaudeville Artists' created by Edward Albee, head of the B.F. Keith circuit in 1916 to oppose *The White Rats*. If an act wanted to work "The Big Time" in America they had to join the N.V.A.
O.P.	Opposite Prompt. The side of the stage on the right of a Performer and the left of the audience.
ORCHESTRA PIT	A section between the stage and the auditorium where the pit orchestra sat. It was lower than the seating in the stalls so that the musicians and their instruments did not obstruct the view of the performance.
PAINT FRAME	Many Vaudeville/Variety Theatres had a large wooden *Frame* at the back of the stage where *Cloths* were stretched for painting. The *Frame* could be raised or lowered by means of a hand winch for the *Scenic Artist* who worked on an elevated platform the full width of the *Cloth*.
PASS DOOR	The door between the auditorium and back-stage. Only the Theatre Manager and Stage Manager were authorised to use the pass-door; however at the famous Metropolitan Theatre, Edgware Road, London agents buzzed to and fro through the pass door, particularly on Monday nights.

PATTER ACT

A comedy talk act between two people. Usually two men or man and woman e.g. Burns and Allen; Ben Lyon and Bebe Daniels. A single comic could just patter which is different from telling *Gags*. e.g. George Jessel with his imaginary phone conversations with his mother.

PERFORMER, THE

The official paper of the Variety Artistes' Federation published weekly in London from 29th March 1906 until 26th September 1957.

PERCH ACT

Form of *Acrobatic Act* where a *Bearer* balances a long pole on the head or shoulder and another performer climbs the pole and performs balances on apparatus at the top of the pole.

PERCH ACT
Les Feuri, 1955

PICCANINNY ACT Enactments of plantation scenes with songs and dances by coloured juveniles were very popular in Vaudeville from 1905 to 1920. e.g. Josephine Gassman and her Piccaninnies or Maud Fanning and her Piccaninnies.

PRESTIDIGITATOR Card manipulator. Form of conjuring using great flexibility of fingers to manipulate cards or billiard balls. A popular frontcloth act.

PRINCIPAL BOY One of the important roles in Pantomime traditionally played by a girl with a fine voice and even finer legs!

PROFILE A piece of scenery, a flat or the edge of a wing, cut out in profile like a tree trunk, cottage etc., used in Pantomimes or Revues.

PROMPT SIDE The left side of the stage for the Performer or the right side looking from the audience. See *Working-Side* and note that the *Working Side* was not always on the *Prompt Side* but the left side of the stage to performers was always called the *Prompt Side*.

PROPS Properties. All sorts of equipment utilised by an Act. Clubs, tables, chairs, all types of gear, etc. It was an unwritten law that no-one ever touched or interfered with another acts props. Most acts preferred to set and strike their own Props. If they used a stagehand to help or to do the job for them that stagehand would expect and receive a gratuity, or if they had to go on stage to help with Props there was an award rate for that called "Appearance Money".

PROS

Short for Professionals. The term used by Vaudeville/Variety Performers to refer to themselves and other Performers in the profession. There was a thinly disguised disdain for those not fully employed in the profession e.g. amateurs and semi-pros.

PROSCENIUM

The frame around the front of the stage which separates the stage from the auditorium. Also called the Proscenium Arch.

PROTEAN ARTISTE

A very versatile performer. Term frequently used by reviewers from 1905 to 1915 for *Character Actors*, particularly those who presented several well known types in rapid succession. See also "quick change act".

QUICK-CHANGE ACT

Sketch Artists or dramatic actors presented Vaudeville/Variety Acts with as many as thirteen lightning quick changes of costume and make-up. The changes were accomplished on stage by moving behind a screen as one character and coming out the other side of the screen as a different character, without any *Stage Wait* at all!

RAKE

The slope of the stage from the back wall towards the footlights. When the large Vaudeville/Variety Theatres were built from 1880 to 1912 the stages were raked in order that the audience seated in the stalls could see the clever dancing feet of the Performers. The rake of some stages was considerable and *Tumblers, Balancers* and *Dancers* had to compensate for the rake in their performance. Modern theatres tend to rake the auditorium instead of the stage.

REAL PRO The highest acclaim from other members of the profession is to be called a "Real Pro". It means one is very professional and performs a first rate Act.

REVOLVE Revolving stage. Some Vaudeville/Variety Theatres e.g. The London Coliseum and the Palace, Leicester had revolving stages or revolves within revolves. Used mainly in big Production Numbers or Magic Acts. Not much used in straight Vaudeville/Variety.

REVOLVING LADDER ACT Usually a two-man Comedy Acrobatic Act. The Performers balanced on the ladder as it revolved and did acrobatic tricks, comedy falls etc.

REVOLVING LADDER ACT:
The Balcombes, 1940s

RISLEY ACT

Juggling of people with the feet. First performed by American Richard Risley Carlisle over a hundred and fifty years ago. The *Bearer* lies on a special piece of apparatus called a *Risley Pad* or *Trinka*, with feet in the air. Acrobats are juggled in the air turning somersaults etc at great speed. e.g. The Kremos early this century and The Seven Ashtons, an Australian Risley Act 1940-1960 both of which were famous on Vaudeville/Variety circuits all over the world. This type of act is sometimes called an Icarien Act.

The Ashtons, 1940s

RISLEY ACTS

The Four Christianis, 1950s

RISER

A *Cloth* or *Gauze* taken up in view of the audience. e.g. in a Revelation Scene in Pantomime.

ROLLER-ACT

Balancing on a board placed across a roller on a high pedestal, juggling rings etc. or featuring head to head, hand to head Balancing. Walthon & Dorraine were a roller act popular in the 1940s and 50s.

ROLLER-ACT

ROLLER BALANCING ACT: *The Stanleys, 1940s*

ROPE SPINNERS

Usually part of a "Western Act" together with *Sharp Shooting* and *Whip Cracking*.

ROSIN BOX

Rosin is an adhesive solid substance obtained after the distillation of turpentine. It is used by *Dancers* and *Acrobats* to prevent slipping on the stage. Boxes with small lumps of rock rosin were placed on either side of the stage and performers crushed the rosin with their shoes just before going on stage. *Aerial Acts* rubbed it on their hands to prevent losing their grip.

ROSTRUM	A raised platform like a small stage, placed on the stage to elevate an act so that it could be seen to greater effect.
ROUTE	The American term for a string of dates on the American/Canadian Vaudeville circuits. Same as a "Tour" of British Variety circuits.
RUNNING ORDER	The list put up by Head Office or the Resident Stage Manager, showing the order in which acts were to appear. It could differ from the printed programme.
RUNNING OVER	For an act to run over the time allowed for their act. A breach of contract and if repeated after one warning the Act could be cancelled.
RUNNING UNDER	For an act to run less than the allotted time. A similar breach of contract. Time was immensely important in Vaudeville/Variety.
SCENA	Pronounced "shay-nah". A scene in a Revue with the chorus, a soubrette, several principals and sometimes a Speciality Act. A big production number usually on some theme e.g. A Spanish scene or a tropical scene.
SEGUE	A direction on music meaning "Follow on at once". As soon as one act finished and took their *Call* the Musical Director would "Segue" into the music of the next act. There were no announcements. Just one act immediately after the other.
SERIO	Female singer of serious and comic songs in Music Hall. Some also danced. Became soubrettes in Revues.

SET	The term applied to a stage arrangement or scene. *To Set* is to arrange the stage by bringing in the appropriate *Cloths* or *Tabs*, *Props* etc. The opposite of *Strike*.
SHARP SHOOTERS	Shooting or Knife Throwing around a human target usually a partner in the act, sometimes part of a "Western Act", also including *Rope Spinning*.
SHOW-DATE	A week at a Variety or Vaudeville Theatre in London or New York where a new act could be seen by agents and bookers. e.g. The Victoria Palace or Grand, Clapham. The act appeared as part of the usual programme, but at a reduced salary of expenses only.
SIFFLEURS	Whistlers. Bird Mimics and Tune Whistlers e.g. Ronnie Ronalde enjoyed popularity 1944-1960.
SINGERS	Male and female from operatic to popular recording artistes. e.g. Count Philipini to Vera Lynn.
SIT-AROUND, THE	The semi-circle of performers used in Minstrel Shows. Sometimes one half of a Vaudeville programme was a Minstrel-type show with performers in a sit-around coming forward to do a short item. It helped save money if business was poor as only half as many acts need be booked to do both parts of the programme. It was sometimes used by Clays and Fullers.
SIZE	Powdered glue, which mixed with boiling water and the powdered paints used for scenery, prevented the paint from rubbing off. It is the prevailing smell backstage as the cloths and backstage dust always retain the odour of the size. Very evocative to all old performers!

SKATING ACTS　　Both Ice and Roller acts carried their own small rinks and appeared on Vaudeville/Variety bills from early this century. Usually a male and female but sometimes a three- or four-handed act.

SKATING ACTS

ROLLER SKATING: *The Heirolls, 1954*

SKETCH-ACTS　　There were many famous *Sketch Acts* in Vaudeville/Variety. e.g. Harry Tate's Motoring sketch still popular on radio.

SKIPS　　Large, square, lined, wicker baskets used for *Props*, *Tabs*, costumes etc. instead of trunks, for transport from one theatre to another.

SKY CLOTH　　A pale blue cloth used as a background for many scenes. It took lighting very well and was used by many acts which worked in silhouette. A standard part of equipment in most theatres. See also Cyclorama.

SOUBRETTE　　Solo singer and dancer in Revues. Usually in front of the chorus.

SPARKS　　Common term for all electricians in theatres.

SPECIALITY ACTS   All the acts in Vaudeville/Variety/Revue and Panto with a highly skilled component. Note the correct spelling and pronunciation. SPEC-IAL-I-TY.

SPLIT WEEK   In America some Vaudeville contracts were for *Split Weeks* of three nights in one theatre and three or four in another theatre sometimes in another town a rail jump away.

SPOTS   Spotlights. See Limes.

SPRINGBOARD ACTS   See Teeter-board.

STAGE-BALANCE   The first thing a young performer learns is to use all the stage and not work just in one spot or on one side.

STAGE-DOOR KEEPER   The guardian of the backstage and dressingroom area. He looked after the keys to dressingrooms, the mail for performers etc and prevented unauthorised persons from entering. He guarded the stage door at all hours the theatre was open.

STAGE HOOKS   Heavy metal hooks which went through holes in the stage to hold guy ropes. Where it was not possible to drill holes in the stage, plates had to be used. see stage plates.

STAGE HOOK: *This slipped through a ¼" hole in the stage. It was approximately 6" long and was used to fix the guy ropes for the 'Web' or aerial acts.*

STAGE PLATES

Metal plates with a removable "shoe" which could hold the shackles to take guy ropes or wires for aerial apparatus or other gear needing secure fixing to the stage. The plates were fixed to the stage with six or eight screws and being flat were able to be left in position. The shoes with shackles and wires could then be slipped into the slots and set and tightened very quickly to avoid *Stage Waits*. As *Stage-Plates* were usually well up-stage or off-stage they did not impede *dancers* or other acts.

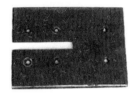

Stage Plate secured to stage by six screws

Shoe for the Stage Plate

STAGE PLATE

Shoe in position to slide into Stage Plate

Shoe in Stage Plate with guy rope attached

STAGE SCREW

A large screw with a hand piece. Used to hold a brace in position. See illustration.

STAGE SCREW

STAGE, THE

The weekly theatrical newspaper published in London since the 25th March 1880 and still going strong. The Stage also published a Year Book from 1908 to 1928; 1949 to 1972; there was a break during the Depression and war years. The Year Books give a comprehensive coverage of all aspects of stage performance. The Stage Guides published in 1912 and 1950-2 list all Variety Theatres with stage sizes, number of dressingrooms, lighting equipment etc.

STAGE WAIT

The unforgivable sin in any performance. To keep an audience waiting between acts because the set hadn't been changed quickly enough or because a performer wasn't ready to go on. In a No 1 theatre heads would roll!!

STANDARD ACT

An act acceptable on the No 1 Vaudeville/Variety circuits around the world.

STOOGE

A comic's assistant usually portraying someone not very bright. Someone from whose actions or lines the comic could get laughs.

STRAIGHTMAN

A Comic's Feed. Likely to be suave and portraying the more intelligent role. See also Feed.

STRIKE

To dismantle a *Set*. To remove it from the stage.

SWAGS

The *Tabs* could be swagged or festooned by means of rings sewn on the back of the curtains and hooks on wires from the flys inserted to pull parts of the *Tabs* up into festoons.

SWITCHBOARD   All lighting in the theatre, with the exception of the *Limes*, was controlled from a *Switchboard* on the side of the stage. The *Switchboard* was usually built on a platform above the *Working Corner* where the Stage Manager and Chief Electrician could keep in close communication during the show.

SWITCHBOARD   *A large theatre switchboard of 1916 installed at the BRISTOL HIPPODROME*

TABS 1	The professional name for curtains. Originally "Tableaux Curtains" which could be drawn off to the sides. Most theatres had at least five sets of different coloured *Tabs* which could be used and lighted in many different ways to ensure that every act had a different setting and that the audience saw different sets every week.
TABS 2	Music played quickly whilst an act took its' "Call" or applause after the "Tabs" closed at the finish of the act.
TANGLE ROUTINE	Highly skilled, silent, comedy routine of becoming entangled in clothing or with microphone cord, etc. Requires great skill and rehearsal to prevent repetition and make it look accidental. e.g. The Bashful Boys and Charles Goll.
TANK ACTS	Large tanks of water on stage for *Diving Acts*, *Swimming Acts* and *Escapologists' Acts* e.g. Houdini and Sea-lion Acts. e.g. Odiva and her Seals.
TAP-MATS	Special mats of wooden slats on a canvas backing were travelled by some *Tap-dancing Acts* to ensure their beats were heard. Some stages were "dead" and did not resound well. The mats were easily rolled for transporting.
TATTY	Term applied to costumes or scenery not fresh and clean. Usually in third-rate Revues.
TAYLORS TRUNKS	Large theatrical *Trunks* made by Taylors of Chicago. Regarded as a status symbol by Vaudevillians.

TEETER-BOARD

Like a long see-saw on a pivot. A heavy acrobat acted as *Jumper* on one end of the board sending a smaller, lighter acrobat high into the air to turn somersaults before landing on the head or shoulders of *Catchers*, sometimes three or four high.

TEETERBOARD ACT

The Great Magyar Troupe, 1935

TENT SHOWS

Touring shows through the country areas of Australia often performed in large tents. Every type of show from Shakespeare to Revues was presented with fit-up stages and scenery in tents. The most famous tent shows were those of George Sorlie. There were some tent shows in small towns in America.

TIMING	Probably the most misused and misunderstood term. *Good Timing* by a comedian or any act is being able to anticipate the audience reaction to a line or trick and wait to deliver the next laugh or trick until just the right time when the laughter or applause starts to fade. It is only acquired with experience. The laughter or·applause is often lost when cut off by the next line. On the other hand· there should not be any discernible pause. The acknowledged *master of Timing* was Max Miller.
TOURS, THE	A list of *Dates* on the big Variety circuits in Britain. e.g. The Moss and Stoll circuits. Equivalent to "Routes" in America.
TRAMPOLINE ACT	The bouncing bed which is quite familiar today. Some acts worked from Trampolines to catchers on trapeze or to other apparatus. Usually Acts of two or three performers.
TRAPS	Different types of Trapdoors in the stage were much in use particularly in Pantomimes and for Magic Acts from the 1880s until 1930s. The "Star" Traps were operated by winches or manually and could project the performer standing on the platform, up through the stage with great force. They are not much in use now.
TRIAL NIGHTS	Acts starting out in the business in Australia could go on at the *Trial Nights*, usually Friday night, on Harry Clay's No 3 theatre circuit in Sydney. The reaction of the audience could be less than enthusiastic for some of the Acts!! Some of the No 2 or 3 Vaudeville Theatres in America had *Trial Nights*; they were also held in some Music Halls.
TROUPER	Used sometimes as a compliment by calling someone "A Real Trouper'. It does not apply to Vaudeville/Variety Artistes who were never in a Troupe but highly individual. Probably derived from seaside Pierrots.

TRUCKS　　　　　　　Scenery on platforms on low wheels which could be quickly and silently wheeled on stage and off.

TRUNKS　　　　　　　When travelling was mainly by rail and ship it was usual for acts to transport their costumes, props etc in large *Trunks*. See *Wardrobe Trunks*.

Taylor's famous 'Professional Trunks'.
Similar to my parent's trunk used for
travelling the 'Web'. About 1912

TUMBLING ACT　　　Troupes of acrobats presenting very fast flip flaps, round off flip flaps, back somersaults, spot tinsikas etc. They filled the stage with flying bodies and were great applause getters.

U.B.O.　　　　　　　The *United Booking Office* was formed by the V.M.A., The *Vaudeville Managers Association* in 1900. It was described as an agency but operated as a monopoly by the managers as it controlled bookings for all the major Vaudeville circuits; Keith; Orpheum; Hammersteins; Polis; Proctor and Sheas. Any act working for the opposition William Morris Agency was blacklisted by the U.B.O. It became very much the baby of Edward Albee for B.F. Keith. Any act wanting to work "The Big Time" in America had to work through the U.B.O.

UNICYCLE ACT   Many types of *Unicycle Acts* with head to head balancing, juggling etc were featured in Vaudeville/Variety.

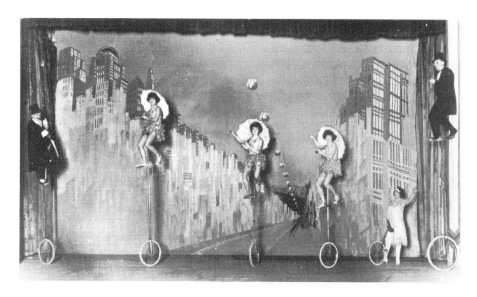

The Pedlars Troupe, 1935

UP AND DOWN FOR TRICKS   An instruction on music of *Speciality Acts* to the *Musical Director* to play softly whilst they perform a difficult trick and then to play loudly when they complete the trick.

UP STAGE   Towards the back of the stage.

UPSTAGE, TO   To work to someone on the stage in a way which forces them to turn upstage away from the audience. In this way their words are lost and they appear to be bad performers.

UTILITY MAN   In Revues a man or woman who worked in scenas, and small parts in sketches etc.

U.V. LIGHTS

Ultra violet light, black-light or *strobolight* was used as a great novelty from the forties. Special *U.V. Lamps*, which were usually placed in the footlights, illuminated U.V. paint on props or special U.V. materials in costumes. The lamps took some time to warm up and needed to be switched on at least ten minutes prior to the act. All other lights had to be switched off before the U.V. light became effective. As it also picked up natural teeth it was necessary to keep one's mouth shut especially if one had some false teeth which did not show up!!! The U.V. colours were brilliant red, green and gold and a few other colours. The white U.V. paint on black tights was used by *Skeleton Acts* because only the bones drawn on the tights were visible. A very effective act.

V.A.B.F.

The Variety Artistes' Benevolent Fund founded in 1907 was the Variety Artistes' own charity. Brinsworth, the Home for Retired Variety Artistes, was opened in 1911. The Royal Variety Performance is staged annually to raise funds to maintain it. It is now called The Entertainment Artistes Benevolent Fund.

V.A.F.

The Variety Artistes' Federation established in London, February 1906 by four performers, Joe O'Gorman, W.H. Clemart, Wal Pink and Fred Russell. By 1914 it was affiliated with The White Rats Actors Union of America; The International Artists' Lodge of Germany; L'Union Syndicate des Artistes Lyriques of France and The Australian Vaudeville Artists' Association. Whilst membership was not compulsory, most Variety Artistes joined because the benefits were numerous. The V.A.F. merged with British Actors' Equity in May 1967 after most Variety Theatres had closed due to the impact of television.

VAMP	To improvise accompaniment. Not something one would ask the orchestra to do in a Number One Theatre even though they could do it very well.
VARIETY	1880-1960. See Napier's Guide to Popular Theatre Before T.V. Also title of largest American weekly theatrical paper.
VAUDEVILLE	1882-1932. See Napier's Guide to Popular Theatre Before T.V.

Vaudeville Bill, 1922 displayed by the compiler

VENT ACT	Ventriloquist. There were an amazing range of Vent Acts. Some with only one "doll" or "dummy" e.g. Fred Russell with Coster Joe; some with many dolls e.g. Arthur Prince. Two famous Vent Acts, G.W. Jester in the 1880s and Senor Wences in the 1940-60 period used the "Talking Hand" with a face drawn on the hand. Others like Walter Lambert had life size dolls.

V.M.A. Vaudeville Managers Association formed in the spring of 1900 by B.F. Keith and Edward Albee to persuade all major Vaudeville Theatres in America to unite under one Booking Office to regulate salaries, dates and routes and to ensure a uniform high standard of Acts. The V.M.A. was replaced by the U.B.O. in 1906. With the reconstruction of Vaudeville after World War One the V.M.A. became the Vaudeville Managers Protective Association when Albee convinced other managers that the profession should be organized on modern lines. Disputes between Artistes and Management were settled by a Joint Arbitration Board known as the "Supreme Court of Vaudeville" representing managers and members of the National Vaudeville Artists Inc.

WALK-DOWN see Finale.

WARDROBE TRUNK A large trunk which opened vertically to reveal a set of five drawers of varying sizes on one side and hanging space on the other side. A useful piece of furniture in the dressingroom and great for travelling costumes without crushing. See illustration.

WATER RATS

The Grand Order of Water Rats, a society for male performers only, founded in London in 1890 to organize social events to raise money for charity. A sister organization, The Lady Ratlings, was formed in 1929.

WEEK OUT

A week without a date or booking.

WEIGHTS

Heavy stage weights in different shapes and sizes used to hold scenery in place. One learnt to avoid stubbing toes or falling over *Stage Weights* in the wings or backstage in blackouts.

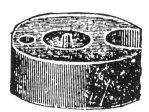

WESTERN ACTS

Rope Spinning, Whip Cracking and *Sharp Shooting* whilst dressed in "Western" costume. These acts became popular in the twenties probably as a result of silent Western films e.g. Tom Mix etc.

WHIP-CRACKERS

Usually part of "Western Acts" with Rope Spinning.

WHITE RATS

The American Vaudeville Artists Association which based its organization on The Water Rats in the U.K. was founded in 1900. It was revitalized by an English act, Harry Mountford, in 1907 and in 1910 he convinced The American Federation of Labor that the Actors National Union was under-written by the managements. The A.F.L. compelled an amalgamation called The White Rats Actors Union on 7th Nov. 1910. The White Rats of America became a branch of this new union. A sister organization, Associated Actresses of America, was formed in 1910.

WIRE ACTS

Tight-wire or *Slack Wire Acts* were popular *Speciality Acts* in Vaudeville/Variety. e.g. Con Colleano. High Wire Acts were not suitable for theatres. They were Circus or Gala Acts.

WIRE ACTS

☙ TIGHT WIRE: *Ron & Rita, 1950s*

JUGGLING ON THE SLACK WIRE: ☙
Jimmy Jeff & June, 1950s

WORKING CORNER The position where the *Stage Manager* stood throughout the performance to cue the flys, supervise the stage staff etc. Note that the Working Corner was not always on the *Prompt Side*. It depended on the design of the theatre, position of dressingrooms, switchboard etc. It was always downstage in the No. One entrance closest to the *house tabs*.

WORKING LIGHT A single 1,000 watt lamp left to light the stage when no performance was in progress.

WOW FINISH The big build-up at the end of an act which brought the applause as the tabs closed.

VALANTYNE NAPIER

*The compiler in her dressing room at
The Metropolitan Theatre, Edgware Road,
London. She is wearing the coat which she
used in her act, Vyne and Valantyne
(see page 8, lower picture).*

EMPIRE THEATRE

PETERBOROUGH : 'Phone 223

MONDAY, AUGUST 18th, 1930
6-35 — TWICE NIGHTLY — 8-40

WONDER WEEK OF VARIETY!

First appearance in Peterboro' of the World Renowned

ANDO FAMILY

7 JAPANESE ENTERTAINERS, in a wonderful Oriental Setting,
Equilibrists, Tumblers, Top Spinning, and the Sensational
" SLIDE FOR LIFE."

BENSON SISTERS

present " A SURPRISE PACKET !"

JACK BOOT & GABY BOLON

In a Novel Comedy Offering

ERNEST SHANNON

The Wireless Star, Mimicry, Mirth and Melody

TOM TAYLOR

The Musical Rustic

THE ZANFRELLAS

'La Pedestal Equipoise'

TODD & SELTZER

Dancers Extraordinary

Pleasing Engagement of

BOB BARLOW

The King of the Road, Singing Vagabond.

A Variety bill of 1930

Forthcoming books from
THE BADGER PRESS
Westbury, Wiltshire

'LOST THEATRES OF DUBLIN'
by Philip B. Ryan
Chapters on each of the lost Theatres, together with
numerous illustrations.

'VARIETY AT NIGHT IS GOOD FOR YOU'
by J.O. Blake
A description of all the London Variety Theatres
open in the 1930s and 1940s with illustrations of the
Theatres, inside and out, by Nicholas Charlesworth.
Also numerous bills of the shows presented.